Dewdrops on a Lotus Leaf

DEWDROPS ON A LOTUS LEAF

Zen Poems of Ryōkan

Translated & edited by
John Stevens

SHAMBHALA
Boston & London
1993

Shambhala Publications, Inc.
Horticultural Hall
300 Massachusetts Avenue
Boston, Massachusetts 02115

9 8 7 6 5 4 3 2 1
First Edition
Printed in the United States of America on acid-free paper ⊗
Distributed in the United States by Random House, Inc.,
and in Canada by Random House of Canada Ltd

Library of Congress Cataloging-in-Publication Data
Ryōkan, 1758–1831.
    [Poems. English. Selections]
    Dewdrops on a lotus leaf: Zen poems of Ryōkan/
translated and edited by John Stevens.—1st ed.
        p. cm.—(Shambhala centaur editions)
    ISBN 0-87773-884-X (alk. paper)
    1. Ryōkan, 1758–1831—Translations into English. 2. Zen
poetry, Japanese—Translations into English. 3. Zen poetry,
Chinese—Translations into English. I. Stevens, John, 1947–
II. Title. III. Series.
PL797.6.A28 1993   93-20221
895.6'134—dc20   CIP

Cover art: "Autumn Leaves," by Ryokan. Ink on decorated paper.
Courtesy of the Takashi Yanagi Collection.

Contents

Translator's Introduction

THE ZEN POET Ryōkan was born in 1758 in the remote and snowy province of Echigō, located in northern Honshū, bordering the Sea of Japan. His father was the village headman and a haiku poet of some note, and Ryōkan received a thorough education in the classics of China and Japan. Shy and studious as a boy, Ryōkan was the local Don Juan for a brief period in his youth. Following a spiritual crisis around the age of twenty, however, he renounced his patrimony and entered a Zen monastery.

In 1780 Ryōkan became the disciple of Kokusen, the top Sōtō Zen *rōshi* of the period, and accompanied that master to Entsū-ji in Tamashima. Ryōkan trained diligently at that lovely little monastery until Kokusen's death in 1791. Even though he had received formal sanction as Kokusen's Dharma heir, Ryōkan spurned all invitations to head up his own temple and embarked instead on a long pilgrimage, wandering all over Japan during the next decade.

In his early forties, Ryōkan drifted back to his native place, and he remained there the rest of his days, living quietly in mountain hermitages. He supported himself by begging, sharing his food with birds and beasts, and spent his time doing Zen meditation, gazing at the moon, playing games with the local children and geisha, visiting friends, drinking rice wine with farmers, dancing at festivals, and composing poems brushed in exquisite calligraphy.

A friend wrote this about Ryōkan:

> When Ryōkan visits it is as if spring had come on a dark winter's day. His character is pure and he is free of duplicity and guile. Ryōkan resembles one of the immortals of ancient literature and religion. He radiates warmth and compassion. He never gets angry, and will not listen to criticism of others. Mere contact with him brings out the best in people.

Once a relative of Ryōkan's asked him to speak to his delinquent son. Ryōkan came to visit the family home but did not say a word of admonition to the boy. He stayed the night and prepared to leave the following morning. As the wayward boy was helping tie Ryōkan's straw sandals, he felt a warm drop of water on his shoulder. Glancing up, the boy saw Ryōkan, with eyes full of tears, looking down at him. Ryōkan departed silently, but the boy soon mended his ways.

The samurai lord of the local domain heard of Ryōkan's reputation as a worthy Zen monk and wanted to construct a temple and install Ryōkan as abbot. The lord went to visit the monk at Gogō-an, Ryōkan's hermitage on Mount Kugami, but he was out gathering flowers, and the party waited patiently until Ryōkan returned with a bowl full of fragrant blossoms. The lord made his request, but

Ryōkan remained silent. Then he brushed a haiku on a piece of paper and handed it to the lord:

> The wind gives me
> Enough fallen leaves
> To make a fire.

The lord nodded in acknowledgment and returned to his castle.

Once, after the long winter confinement, Ryōkan visited the village barber to have his shaggy head of hair shaved off. The barber cut one side but then demanded a ransom to finish the job: a sample of Ryōkan's calligraphy. Ryōkan brushed the name of a Shintō god, a kind of calligraphy that served as a good-luck charm. Pleased that he had outwitted the monk, the barber had the calligraphy mounted and displayed it in his alcove.

A visitor remarked to the barber one day, "You know, there is a character missing from the god's name."

Such an omission negates the calligraphy's effect as a talisman, and the barber confronted Ryōkan. Ryōkan scolded him good-naturedly for his greed: "You short-changed me, so I short-changed you. That kind old lady down the road always gives me extra bean cake, so the calligraphy I gave her has an extra character in it!"

Old and infirm, Ryōkan was finally obliged to leave his mountain hut and spent his final days at the home of one of his patrons in the village. Near the end of his life, he fell in love with the beautiful young nun Teishin. She was at Ryōkan's side when he passed away on January 6, 1831, at age seventy-three.*

Ryōkan wrote thousands of poems and poem-letters, both Chinese and Japanese style, and scattered them about. These were treasured by the local folk and later lovingly studied and collected by scholars. The first edition of Ryōkan's poems, titled *Hachisu no Tsuyu* ("Dewdrops on a Lotus Leaf") and compiled by Teishin, appeared in 1835. Expanded

---

*For a detailed biography of Ryōkan, see John Stevens, *Three Zen Masters: Ikkyū, Hakuin, Ryōkan* (Kodansha, 1993). Other editions of Ryōkan's poems in English translation include: Jacob Fischer, *Dew-drops on a Lotus Leaf* (Tokyo: Kenkyūsha, 1954); John Stevens, *One Robe, One Bowl: The Zen Poetry of Ryōkan* (Tokyo: John Weatherhill, 1977); Burton Watson, *Ryōkan: Zen Monk-Poet of Japan* (New York: Columbia University Press, 1981); and Nobuyuki Yuasa, *The Zen Poems of Ryōkan* (New Jersey: Princeton University Press, 1981).

collections of Ryōkan's work have continued to be published over the years, and he is likely Japan's most popular and beloved Zen poet. As mentioned in the tale above, Ryōkan's delightful brushwork, totally unaffected and free-flowing, is also highly esteemed, and Ryōkan is venerated as one of the greatest calligraphers of all time in East Asia.

The practice of Zen and the appreciation of Zen art is now universal, and Ryōkan's life and spirit speak to lovers of poetry, religion, and beauty everywhere. The selection of poems presented here reflects the range and depth of Ryōkan's Zen vision. He focused on "things deep inside the heart," and his poems cover the spectrum of human experience: joy and sadness, pleasure and pain, enlightenment and illusion, love and loneliness, man and nature. Like those of his counterpart Cold Mountain (Han-shan), the legendary Zen poet of T'ang China, Ryōkan's poems reveal the full, rich texture of Zen.

> Good friends and excellent teachers—
> Stick close to them!
> Wealth and power are fleeting dreams
> But wise words perfume the world for ages.

Dewdrops on a Lotus Leaf

Who says my poems are poems?
My poems are not poems.
When you know that my poems are not
    poems,
Then we can speak of poetry!

It's a pity, a gentleman in refined retirement
    composing poetry:
He models his work on the classic verse of
    China,
And his poems are elegant, full of fine
    phrases.
But if you don't write of things deep inside
    your own heart,
What's the use of churning out so many
    words?

When I was a lad,
I sauntered about town as a gay blade,
Sporting a cloak of the softest down,
And mounted on a splendid chestnut-colored
  horse.
During the day, I galloped to the city;
At night, I got drunk on peach blossoms by
  the river.
I never cared about returning home,
Usually ending up, with a big smile on my
  face, at a pleasure pavilion!

Thinking back, I recall my days at Entsū-ji
And the solitary struggle to find the Way.
Carrying firewood reminded me of Layman
    Hō;
When I polished rice, the Sixth Patriarch
    came to mind.
I was always first in line to receive the
    Master's teaching,
And never missed an hour of meditation.
Thirty years have flown by since
I left the green hills and blue sea of that
    lovely place.
What has become of all my fellow disciples?
And how can I forget the kindness of my
    beloved teacher?
The tears flow on and on, blending with the
    swirling mountain stream.

Returning to my native village after many
   years' absence:
Ill, I put up at a country inn and listen to the
   rain.
One robe, one bowl is all I have.
I light incense and strain to sit in meditation;
All night a steady drizzle outside the dark
   window—
Inside, poignant memories of these long years
   of pilgrimage.

   Layman Hō (Chinese, P'ang) was a Zen master of the T'ang era.
One of his famous sayings was "Miraculous power, marvelous activity:
drawing water, chopping wood." *The Sixth Patriarch* refers to Enō
(Hui-neng, 638–717), who once worked as a rice polisher in a monastery.

To my Teacher

An old grave hidden away at the foot of a
  deserted hill,
Overrun with rank weeds growing unchecked
  year after year;
There is no one left to tend the tomb,
And only an occasional woodcutter passes by.
Once I was his pupil, a youth with shaggy
  hair,
Learning deeply from him by the Narrow
  River.
One morning I set off on my solitary journey
And the years passed between us in silence.
Now I have returned to find him at rest here;
How can I honor his departed spirit?
I pour a dipper of pure water over his
  tombstone

And offer a silent prayer.
The sun suddenly disappears behind the hill
And I'm enveloped by the roar of the wind in
  the pines.
I try to pull myself away but cannot;
A flood of tears soaks my sleeves.

In my youth I put aside my studies
And I aspired to be a saint.
Living austerely as a mendicant monk,
I wandered here and there for many springs.
Finally I returned home to settle under a
  craggy peak.
I live peacefully in a grass hut,
Listening to the birds for music.
Clouds are my best neighbors.
Below, a pure spring where I refresh body
  and mind;
Above, towering pines and oaks that provide
  shade and brushwood.
Free, so free, day after day—
I never want to leave!

If someone asks
My abode
I reply:
"The east edge of
The Milky Way."

Like a drifting cloud,
Bound by nothing:
I just let go
Giving myself up
To the whim of the wind.

Torn and tattered, torn and tattered,
Torn and tattered is this life.
Food? I collect it from the roadside.
The shrubs and bushes have long overrun
    my hut.
Often the moon and I sit together all night,
And more than once I lost myself among
    wildflowers, forgetting to return home.
No wonder I finally left the community life:
How could such a crazy monk live in a
    temple?

Two Poems for My Friend Bōsai

Yes, I'm truly a dunce
Living among trees and plants.
Please don't question me about illusion and
    enlightenment—
This old fellow just likes to smile to himself.
I wade across streams with bony legs,
And carry a bag about in fine spring weather.
That's my life,
And the world owes me nothing.

The gaudy beauty of this world has no
    attraction for me—
My closest friends are mountains and rivers,
Clouds swallow up my shadow as I walk
    along,
When I sit on cliffs, birds soar overhead.

Wearing snowy straw sandals, I visit cold
   villages.
Go as deep as you can into life,
And you will be able to let go of even
   blossoms.

Kameda Bōsai (1752–1826), a famous scholar, artist, and poet of the
Edō Period, visited Ryōkan in Echigō.

A single path among ten thousand trees,
A misty valley hidden among a thousand
  peaks.
Not yet autumn but already leaves are falling;
Not much rain but still the rocks grow dark.
With my basket I hunt for mushrooms;
With my bucket I draw pure spring water.
Unless you got lost on purpose
You would never get this far.

I climb to Great Compassion Hall
And gaze out at the clouds and haze.
Ancient trees stretch toward the sky,
A fresh breeze whispers of ten thousand
    generations.
Below, Dragon King Spring—
So pure you can see right to its source.
To passersby I shout,
"Come and see yourself mirrored in the
    water!"

In the stillness by the empty window
I sit in formal meditation wearing my monk's
    surplice.
Navel and nose in alignment,
Ears parallel with the shoulders.
Moonlight floods the room;
The rain stops but the eaves drip and drip.
Perfect this moment—
In the vast emptiness, my understanding
    deepens.

At night, deep in the mountains,
I sit in meditation.
The affairs of men never reach here:
Everything is quiet and empty,
All the incense has been swallowed up by
 the endless night.
My robe has become a garment of dew.
Unable to sleep, I walk out into the woods—
Suddenly, above the highest peak, the full
 moon appears.

In my hermitage a volume of *Cold Mountain Poems*—
It is better than any sutra.
I copy his verses and post them all around,
Savoring each one, over and over.

When all thoughts
Are exhausted
I slip into the woods
And gather
A pile of shepherd's purse.

Like the little stream
Making its way
Through the mossy crevices
I, too, quietly
Turn clear and transparent.

Orchid

Deep in the valley, a beauty hides:
Serene, peerless, incomparably sweet.
In the still shade of the bamboo thicket
It seems to sigh softly for a lover.

The Lotus

First blooming in the Western Paradise,
The lotus has delighted us for ages.
Its white petals are covered with dew,
Its jade green leaves spread out over the
    pond,
And its pure fragrance perfumes the wind.
Cool and majestic, it rises from the murky
    water.
The sun sets behind the mountains
But I remain in the darkness, too captivated
    to leave.

Bamboo

The thick bamboo grove near my hut
Keeps me nice and cool.
Shoots proliferate, blocking the path,
While old branches reach for the sky.
Years of frost give bamboo spirit;
They are most mysterious when wrapped in
    mist.
Bamboo is as hardy as pine and oak,
And more subtle than peach or plum
    blossoms.
It grows straight and tall,
Empty inside but with a sturdy root.
I love the purity and honesty of my bamboo,
And want them to thrive here always!

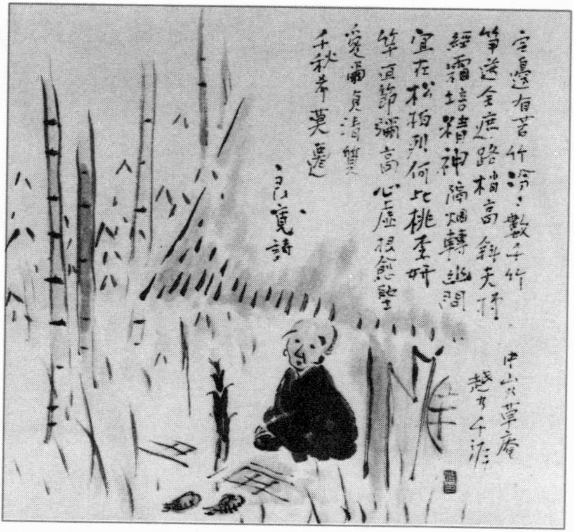

Wild peonies
Now at their peak
In glorious full bloom:
Too precious to pick,
Too precious not to pick.

O lonely pine!
I'd gladly give you
My straw hat and
Thatched coat
To ward off the rain.

In my garden
I raised bush clover,
suzuki grass,
violets, dandelions,
flowery silk trees,
banana plants, morning glories,
boneset, asters,
spiderwort, daylilies:
Morning and evening,
Cherishing them all,
Watering, nourishing,
Protecting them from the sun.
Everyone said my plants
Were at their best.
But on the twenty-fifth of May,
At sunset,
A violent wind

Howled madly,
Battering and rending my plants;
Rain poured down,
Pounding the vines and flowers
Into the earth.
It was so painful
But as the work of the wind
I have to let it be . . .

The plants and flowers
I raised about my hut
I now surrender
To the will
Of the wind.

The flower invites the butterfly with
    no-mind;
The butterfly visits the flower with no-mind.
The flower opens, the butterfly comes;
The butterfly comes, the flower opens.
I don't know others,
Others don't know me.
By not-knowing we follow nature's course.

My hermitage is home to a cat and a mouse;
Both are furry creatures.
The cat is fat and sleeps in broad daylight;
The mouse is thin and scampers about in
    the dark.
The cat is blessed with talent,
Able to deftly catch living things for its
    meals.
The mouse is cursed,
Limited to sneaking bits and pieces of food.
A mouse can damage containers, it is true,
But containers can be replaced,
Not so living things.
If you ask me which creature incurs more sin,
I'd say the cat!

My daily fare: playing with the village
    children.
I've always got a few cloth balls tucked in
    my sleeves:
Not good for much else,
I do know how to enjoy the tranquillity of
    spring!

This cloth ball in my sleeve is more valuable
    than a thousand pieces of gold;
I'm quite skillful at ball playing, you know.
If someone wants to learn my secret, here
    it is:
    "One, two, three, four, five, six, seven!"

袖裏繡毬直千金
謂言好手無等匹
箇中意旨若相問
一二三四五六七

良寛詩
こゝ尓雅

What is this life of mine?
Rambling on, I entrust myself to fate.
Sometimes laughter, sometimes tears.
Neither a layman nor a monk.
An early spring rain drizzles on and on.
But the plum blossoms have yet to brighten
    things up.
All morning I sit by the hearth,
No one to talk to.
I search for my copybook
And then brush a few poems.

A Visit to Mr. Fuji's Villa

It's several miles outside the town
And I walked there together with a
   woodsman
Along a meandering footpath through rows
   of verdant pines.
In the valley around us, sweet-smelling wild
   plum blossoms.
Every time I visit, I gain something new,
And there I feel truly at ease.
The fish in his pond are big as dragons,
And the surrounding forest is still the day
   long.
The inside of his home is full of treasures:
Volumes of books scattered about!
Inspired, I loosen my robe, browse through
   the books,

And then compose my own verse.
At twilight I walk along the eastern corridor
Where I'm greeted again by a little flock of
spring birds.

Summer Evening

The night advances toward dawn,
Dew drips from the bamboo onto my
   brushwood gate.
My neighbor to the west has stopped
   pounding his mortar;
My little hermit's garden grows moist.
Frogs croak near and far,
Fireflies flit high and low.
Wide awake, it's not possible to sleep
   tonight.
I smooth my pillow and let my thoughts
   drift.

Visiting Cloud Peak
with Priest Tenge in Fall

Human existence in this world:
Duckweed cast adrift on the water.
Who can ever feel secure?
That is the reason
I took up a monk's staff, left my parents,
And bade farewell to my friends.
A single patched robe
And one bowl have sustained me all these
    years.
I'm fond of this little hut
And often spend time here—
We are two kindred spirits,
Never worrying about who is guest or host.
The wind blows through lofty pines,

Frost chills the few mums that remain.
Arm in arm we stand above the clouds;
Bound as one, roaming in the far beyond.

At dusk
I often climb
To the peak of Kugami.
Deer bellow,
Their voices
Soaked up by
Piles of maple leaves
Lying undisturbed at
The foot of the mountain.

The Autumn Moon

The moon appears in every season, it is true,
But surely it's best in fall.
In autumn, mountains loom and water runs
    clear.
A brilliant disk floats across the infinite sky,
And there is no sense of light and darkness,
For everything is permeated with its presence.
The boundless sky above, the autumn chill on
    my face.
I take my precious staff and wander about the
    hills.
Not a speck of the world's dust anywhere,
Just the brilliant beams of moonlight.
I hope others, too, are gazing on this moon
    tonight,
And that it's illuminating all kinds of people.

Autumn after autumn, the moonlight comes
   and goes;
Human beings will gaze upon it for eternity.
The sermons of Buddha, the preaching of
   Enō,
Surely occurred under the same kind of
   moon.
I contemplate the moon through the night,
As the stream settles, and white dew
   descends.
Which wayfarer will bask in the moonlight
   longest?
Whose home will drink up the most moon-
   beams?

Shut up among the solitary peaks,
I sadly contemplate the driving sleet outside.
A monkey's cry echoes through the dark hills,
A frigid stream murmurs below,
And the light by the window looks frozen
    solid.
My inkstone, too, is ice-cold.
No sleep tonight, I'll write poems,
Warming the brush with my breath.

On a bitterly cold November night
The snow fell thick and fast—
First like hard grains of salt,
Then more like soft willow buds.
The flakes settled quietly on the bamboo
And piled up pleasingly on the pine branches.
Rather than turning to old texts, the darkness
Makes me feel like composing my own verse.

This world:
A fading
Mountain echo,
Void and
Unreal.

Within
A light snow
Three Thousand Realms;
Within those realms
Light snow falls.

As the snow
Engulfs my hut
At dusk
My heart, too,
Is completely consumed.

Blending with the wind,
Snow falls;
Blending with the snow,
The wind blows.
By the hearth
I stretch out my legs,
Idling my time away
Confined in this hut.
Counting the days,
I find that February, too,
Has come and gone
Like a dream.

An easterly wind brought needed rain
That poured over the thatched roof all night
While this hermit dozed peacefully,
Untroubled by the floating world's agitation.
Green mountains bathe in the sunrise,
Spring birds twitter in the branches.
Aimlessly, I stroll out the gate—
Riverlets flow toward distant villages,
Lovely flowers decorate the slopes.
I spot an old farmer leading an ox
And a youngster carrying a hoe.
Human beings must work in all seasons,
    sunrise to sunset.
I'm the only one with nothing to do,
Sticking close to my native place.

Haiku

I must go there today—
Tomorrow the plum blossoms
Will scatter.

A nightingale's song
Brings me out of a dream:
The morning glows.

A single wish:
To sleep one night
Beneath the cherry blossoms.

The mountain village:
Swallowed up by
A chorus of croaking frogs!

Autumn's first drizzle:
How delightful,
The nameless mountain.

Left behind by the thief—
The moon
In the window.

Around my shuttered door,
Fallen pine needles:
How lonely I feel . . .

Calling out to me
As they return home:
Wild geese at night.

This old body of mine:
A bamboo buried
In the cold snow.

Buddhist Begging

Early on the first of August
I take my bowl and head for town.
Silver clouds accompany my steps,
A golden breeze caresses the bell on my staff.
Ten thousand doors, a thousand gates open
    for me.
I feast my eyes on cool groves of bamboo
    and banana trees.
I beg here and there, east and west,
Stopping at sake shops and fishmongers, too.
An honest gaze can disarm a mountain of
    swords;
A steady stride can glide over the fires of hell.
This was the message the Prince of Beggars
Taught to his top disciples over twenty-seven
    hundred years ago,

And I still act as one of Buddha's
  descendants.
A wise old fellow once said,
"Regarding food, all is equal in the Buddha's
  Law."
Keep those words in mind
No matter how many aeons may pass.

For our sakes
The clams and fish
Give themselves
Unselfishly
As food.

In my little begging bowl
Violets and dandelions,
Mixed together
As an offering to the
Buddhas of the Three Worlds.

Picking violets
By the roadside
I absent-mindedly
Left my little bowl behind—
O poor little bowl!

I've forgotten my
Little begging bowl again—
No one will take you,
Surely no one will take you:
My sad little bowl!

Spring rains,
Summer showers,
A dry autumn:
May nature smile on us
And we all will share in the bounty.

Please don't mistake me
For a bird
When I swoop
Into your garden
To eat the cherry apples.

I went there
To beg rice
But the blooming bush clover
Among the stones
Made me forget the reason.

Along the hedge a few branches of golden
    mums;
Winter crows soar above the thick woods.
A thousand peaks glow brilliantly in the
    sunset,
And this monk returns home with a full
    bowl.

No luck today on my mendicant rounds;
From village to village I dragged myself.
At sunset I find myself with miles of
    mountains between me and my hut.
The wind tears at my frail body,
And my little bowl looks so forlorn—
Yet this is my chosen path that guides me
Through disappointment and pain, cold and
    hunger.

今日も亦逢驟雨

こしの午逸
[印]

After gathering firewood in the mountains
I returned to my hut
And found pickled plums and potatoes
Left beneath my window by a visitor.
The plums were wrapped in paper,
The potatoes in green grass,
And a scrap of paper bore the donor's name.
Deep in the mountains the food is tasteless—
Mostly turnips and greens—
So I quickly boiled the treat with soya paste
    and salt.
I filled my usually empty stomach
With three big bowls.
If my poet friend had left some rice wine
It would have been a real banquet.
I savored about a fifth of the gift and stored
    the rest;

Patting my full belly, I went back to my
     chores.
Buddha's Enlightenment Day will be here in
     six days
And I did not know what to offer
But now I have become rich—
Buddha will feast on plums and delicious
     potato gruel.

A Gift of Seven Pomegranates

Splitting them,
Picking them apart,
Breaking them in two:
Eating, eating, eating—
Not letting them out of my mouth!

Two Poem-Letters

The weather is good and
I have many visitors
But little food.
Any pickled plums
To spare?

It has grown chill
And the firefly
Glows no longer:
Will some kind soul
Send me golden water?

"Firefly" was one of Ryōkan's nicknames. "Golden water" is rice
wine.

My Cracked Wooden Bowl

This treasure was discovered in a bamboo
  thicket—
I washed the bowl in a spring and then
  mended it.
After morning meditation, I take my gruel
  in it;
At night, it serves me soup or rice.
Cracked, worn, weather-beaten, and
  misshapen
But still of noble stock!

To My New Vase

From now on
You'll never be bothered
By even a speck of dust;
Day and night in my care
You'll never be lonely!

Noisy crickets now own the harvested fields;
Bundles of smoldering rice straw fill the plain
    with haze.
Farmers sit by their hearths enjoying the long
    evenings,
Weaving mats and preparing for spring.
When farm families gather and talk
The words "false" and "true" are never
    uttered.
City folk aren't that lucky—
Those poor souls must bow and scrape all
    day.

The year will be over soon,
But I'm still here in my little hut.
Cold autumn rain falls sadly,
And leaves pile up on the temple steps.
I pass time absent-mindedly reading sutras
And chanting some old poems.
Suddenly a child appears and says,
"Come, let's go to the village together."

Poems Exchanged between Ryōkan and His Brother Yoshiyuki

"I hear you play marbles with the brothel girls."

The black robed monk
Sports with
Pleasure girls—
What can be
In his heart?

—from Yoshiyuki

Sporting and sporting,
As I pass through this floating world:
Finding myself here,

Is it not good
To dispel the bad dreams of others?

—RYŌKAN

Sporting and sporting
While passing through this world
Is good, perhaps,
But don't you think of
The world to come?

—YOSHIYUKI

It is in this world,
With this body
That I sport:
No need to think
About the world to come.

—RYŌKAN

Midsummer—
I walk about with my staff.
Old farmers spot me
And call me over for a drink.
We sit in the fields
Using leaves for plates.
Pleasantly drunk and so happy
I drift off peacefully
Sprawled out on a paddy bank.

What luck! I found a coin in my bag!
Now I can call on my friend nicknamed the
    Sleeping Dragon.
I've wanted to drink with him for ages
But lacked the means until now.

For Keizan,
Abbot of Ganjō-ji

Ganjō-ji is west of Hokke-dō, a temple
Secluded among rocks and hidden by thick
  mist.
In the deep valley, moss grows rampant and
  visitors are rarely seen.
Fishes dance in an ancient pond,
Tall pines reach toward the blue sky,
And between the trees a glimpse of Mount
  Yahiko.
One bright September day, on my begging
  rounds,
I impulsively decided to knock on the temple
  gate.
I'm a free-spirited Zen vagrant,

And the abbot, too, has lots of time to spare.
We stayed together all day, not a care in the
   world,
Sipping wine, toasting the mountains, and
   laughing ourselves silly!

Enjoying Rice Wine with
My Younger Brother Yoshiyuki

Older and younger brother together again,
But now both of us have bushy white
  eyebrows.
It's a time of peace and happiness in the
  world,
And day after day we get drunk as fools!

In this world
If there were one
Of a like mind—
We could spend the night
Talking in my little hut!

How can I possibly sleep
This moonlit evening?
Come, my friends,
Let's sing and dance
All night long.

Stretched out,
Tipsy,
Under the vast sky:
Splendid dreams
Beneath the cherry blossoms.

Wild roses,
Plucked from fields,
Full of croaking frogs:
Float them in your wine
And enjoy every minute!

Late at night I draw my inkstone close;
Flushed with wine, I put my worn brush to
    paper.
I want my brushwork to bear the same
    fragrance as plum blossoms,
And even though old I will try harder than
    anyone.

Li Po

After a promenade in the green fields,
   accompanied by a spring wind,
Li Po naps peacefully by his desk.
My host asked to inscribe a painting of
   the poet—
That's easy since I love wine as much as
   Li Po did!

Tu Fu

Enchanted by blossoms, beguiled by willows,
    Tu Fu hid out in a deep valley.
Mounted on a horse, he roamed about,
    gloriously drunk.
In his dreams, he found himself back at
    court,
Dashing off poems for the emperor's
    edification.

    Li Po (701–762) and Tu Fu (712–770) were the two greatest poets
of T'ang China.

Brush and Inkstone

How is my karma related to the brush and
    inkstone?
Over and over I write and write.
The only one who really knows the reason
Is the Great Hero Buddha.

The districts of Echigō are full of beauties,
And today a group of lovelies sport along a
   river greener than brocade.
Hair finely dressed with white jade hairpins;
Delicate hands revealing just a glimpse of
   scarlet undergowns.
The maidens braid grass into garlands as gifts
   for young lords,
And gather branches of flowers as they flirt
   with passersby.
Yet this charming coquetry is melancholy
   somehow,
For it won't outlast their songs and laughter.

The courtesans are turned out in their
    best—
How delightfully they speak and laugh
Along the lovely green river.
They call out to gentlemen the day long
And tempt them with songs that charm the
    hardest heart.
They mince about with flirtatious glances so
    difficult to resist.
Someday, though, even these captivating
    women will have nothing left,
And they will be left out in the harsh cold.

Spring sunset, a willowy miss of sixteen
Returns home with an armful of mountain
    blossoms.
A drizzle caresses her flowers.
She turns heads as she goes by,
Her kimono held up with a slight hitch.
People ask each other:
"Whose daughter is that?"

Long ago, a pretty girl lived next door:
She used to pick mulberries in a distant
   grove,
Returning with her white arms full of
Gold and silver branches.
She sang with a heart-rending voice
And sparkled with life.
Young farmers put aside their hoes when they
   saw her,
And many forgot to return home when she
   was around.
Now she is just a white-haired granny,
Burdened with the aches and pains of
   old age.

Time passes,
There is no way
We can hold it back—
Why, then, do thoughts linger on,
Long after everything else is gone?

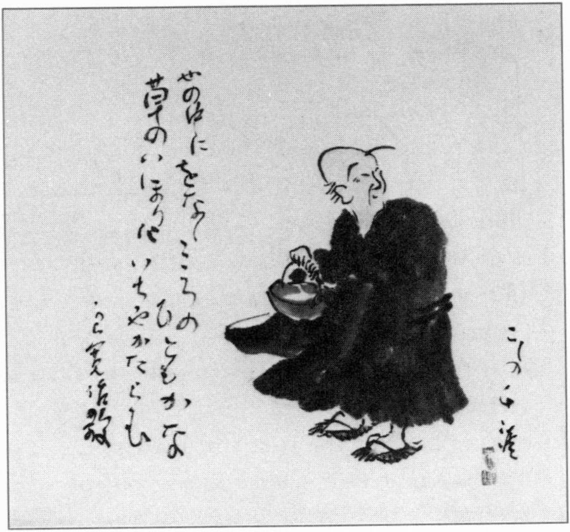

Poem Composed Following
a Terrible Earthquake

Day after day after day,
At noon and midnight, the cold was piercing.
The sky was thick with black clouds that
  blocked out the sun.
Fierce winds howled, snow swirled violently.
Wild waves stormed heaven, buffeting
  monster fish.
Walls trembled and shook, people shrieked in
  terror.
Looking back at the past forty years,
I now see that things were racing out of
  control:
People had grown lax and indifferent,
Forming factions and fighting among
  themselves.

They forgot about obligations and duty,
Ignored notions of loyalty and justice,
And only thought of themselves.
Full of self-conceit, they cheated each other,
Creating an endless, filthy mess.
The world was rife with madness,
No one shared my concern.
Things got worse until the final disaster
    struck—
Few were aware that the world was star-
    crossed
And dreadfully out of kilter.
If you really want to understand this tragedy,
    look deep inside
Rather than helplessly bemoan your cruel
    fate.

Leave off your mad rush for gold and
  jewels—
I've got something far more precious for you:
A bright pearl that sparkles more brilliantly
  than the sun and moon
And illuminates each and every eye.
Lose it and you'll wallow in a sea of pain;
Find it and you'll safely reach the other shore.
I'd freely present this treasure to anyone
But hardly anyone asks for it.

For Hachisuke, an Untouchable

Gold and silver, status and power, all return
   to heaven and earth.
Profit and loss, having and lacking, are all
   essentially empty.
Aristocrats and peasants, saints and sinners,
   end up the same.
We are bound by fate to the whirl of
   existence.
How lamentable, the Beggar of Ryōgoku
   Bridge
Who perished in a dreadful flood.
If you ask me his whereabouts, I'll reply:
"In the heart of the moon's reflection on the
   waves!"

For Children Killed in a Smallpox Epidemic

When spring arrives
From every tree tip
Flowers will bloom,
But those children
Who fell with last autumn's leaves
Will never return.

Keep your heart clear and transparent
And you will never be bound.
A single disturbed thought, though,
Creates ten thousand distractions.
Let myriad things captivate you
And you'll go further and further astray.
How painful to see people
All wrapped up in themselves.

I watch people in the world
Throw away their lives lusting after things,
Never able to satisfy their desires,
Falling into deep despair
And torturing themselves.
Even if they get what they want
How long will they be able to enjoy it?
For one heavenly pleasure
They suffer ten torments of hell,
Binding themselves more firmly to the
    grindstone.
Such people are like monkeys
Frantically grasping for the moon in the
    water
And then falling into a whirlpool.
How endlessly those caught up in the floating
    world suffer.

Despite myself, I fret over them all night
And cannot staunch my flow of tears.

Sometimes I sit quietly,
Listening to the sound of falling leaves.
Peaceful indeed is the life of a monk,
Cut off from all worldly matters.
Then why do I shed these tears?

I'm so aware
That it's all unreal:
One by one, the things
Of this world pass on.
But why do I still grieve?

When I think
About the misery
Of those in this world
Their sadness
Becomes mine.

Oh, that my monk's robe
Were wide enough
To gather up all
The suffering people
In this floating world.

Nothing makes me
More happy than
Amida Buddha's Vow
To save
Everyone.

If you are not put off
By the voice of the valley
And the starry peaks,
Why not walk through the shady cedars
And come see me?

At dusk
Come to my hut—
The crickets will
Serenade you, and I will
Introduce you to the moonlit woods.

To a Visitor

Listen to the cicadas in treetops near the
  waterfall;
See how last night's rains have washed away
  all grime.
Needless to say, my hut is as empty as can
  be,
But I can offer you a window full of the most
  intoxicating air!

For My Visitors

Deep in the woods,
Holed up for the winter
An old fellow like me—
Who will be the first to visit?
I knew it would be you!

During a lull in the rain
I picked some
Wild parsley
For you to enjoy
During your visit.

How heartless
For the snowflakes
Not to fall

On the day
Of your esteemed visit.

Wait for moonlight
Before you go—
The mountain trail
Is thick with
Chestnut burrs!

Reply to a Friend's Letter

Your smoky village is not so far from here
But icy rain kept me captive all morning.
Just yesterday, it seems, we passed an evening
    together discussing poetry
But it's really been twenty windblown days.
I've begun to copy the text you lent me,
Fretting how weak I've become.
This letter seals my promise to take my staff
And make my way through the steep cliffs
As soon as the sun melts the ice along the
    mossy path.

My Precepts

Take care not to:
talk too much
talk too fast
talk without being asked to
talk gratuitously
talk with your hands
talk about worldly affairs
talk back rudely
argue
smile condescendingly at others' words
use elegant expressions
boast
avoid speaking directly
speak with a knowing air
jump from topic to topic
use fancy words

speak of past events that cannot be changed
speak like a pedant
avoid direct questions
speak ill of others
speak grandly of enlightenment
carry on while drunk
speak in an obnoxious manner
yell at children
make up fantastic stories
speak while angry
name-drop
ignore the people to whom you are speaking
speak sanctimoniously of gods and buddhas
use sugary speech
use flattering speech
speak of things of which you have no
    knowledge
monopolize the conversation

talk about others behind their backs
speak with conceit
bad-mouth others
chant prayers ostentatiously
complain about the amount of alms
give long-winded sermons
speak affectedly like an artist
speak affectedly like a tea master

The *I Ching* States Happiness Lies in the Proper Blend of:

Hot-cold
good-bad
black-white
beautiful-ugly
large-small
wisdom-foolishness
long-short
brightness-darkness
high-low
partial-whole
relaxation-quickness
increase-decrease
purity-filth
slow-fast.

Buddha's Path

This is the Way he traveled to flee the
    world;
This is the Way he traveled to return to the
    world.
I, too, come and go along this Sacred Path
That bridges life and death
And traverses illusion.

The ancient buddhas taught the Dharma
Not for its own sake but to assist us.
If we really knew ourselves
We would not have to rely on old teachers.
The wise go right to the core
And leap beyond appearances;
The foolish cleave to details
And get ensnared by words and letters.
Such people envy the accomplishments of
    others
And work feverishly to attain the same things.
Cling to truth and it becomes falsehood;
Understand falsehood and it becomes truth.
Truth and falsehood are two sides of a coin:

Neither accept nor reject either one.
Don't waste your precious time fruitlessly
Trying to gauge the depths of life's ups and
  downs.

When I see learned priests lecturing on the
   sutras
Their eloquence seems to flow in circles:
The Five Periods of the Law and the Eight
   Doctrines—
Nice theories, but who needs them?
Pedants have swelled heads
But ask them matters of real importance
And all you get is empty babble.

Even if you consume as many books
As the sands of the Ganges
It is not as good as really catching
One verse of Zen.
If you want the secret of Buddhism,
Here it is: Everything is in the Heart!

Priest Senkei, a true man of the Way!
He worked in silence—no extra words for
  him.
For thirty years he stayed in Kokusen's
  community.
He never did meditation, never read the
  sutras,
And never said a word about Buddhism,
Just worked for the good of all.
I saw him but did not really see him;
I met him but did not really meet him.
Ah, he is impossible to imitate.
Priest Senkei, a true man of the Way!

Buddha proclaimed countless teachings,
Each one revealing the purest truth.
Just as each breeze and every drop of rain
Refreshes the forest,
There is no sutra that does not lead to
    salvation.
Grasp the essence of each branch
And stop trying to rank Buddha's teaching.

The Great Way leads nowhere,
And it is no place.
Affirm it and you miss it by a mile;
"This is delusion, that is enlightenment" is
    also wide of the mark.
You can expound theories of "existence" and
    "nonexistence"
Yet even talk of the "Middle Way" can get
    you sidetracked.
I'll just keep my wonderful experiences to
    myself.
Babble about enlightenment, and your words
    get torn to shreds.

The wind has settled, the blossoms have
    fallen;
Birds sing, the mountains grow dark—
This is the wondrous power of Buddhism.

In Otogo Forest beneath Mount Kugami
You'll find the tiny hut where I pass my days.
Still no temples or villas for me!
I'd rather live with the fresh breezes and the
  bright moon,
Playing with the village children or making
  poems.
If you ask about me, you'll probably say,
"What is that foolish monk doing now?"

Zen Dialogue in a Dream

I was in town begging when I met an old
   sage:
"Monk, why do you live in the cloud-covered
   peaks?"
"Old fellow," I countered, "why do you
   remain in this dusty place?"
We both wanted to reply but neither of us
   spoke.
Then my reverie was shattered by the sound
   of the temple bell.

I sat facing you for hours but you didn't
   speak;
Then I finally understood the unspoken
   meaning.
Removed from their covers, books lay
   scattered about;
Outside the bamboo screen, rain beats against
   the plum tree.

Dreaming of Saichi,
My Long-Deceased Disciple

I met you again after more than twenty years,
On a rickety bridge, beneath the hazy moon,
   in the spring wind.
We walked on and on, arm in arm, talking
   and talking,
Until suddenly we were in front of Hachiman
   Shrine!

Inscription on
My Painting of a Skull

All things born of karma disappear when
    that karma is exhausted,
But where is this karma born?
From whence does the First Cause arise?
Here words and thoughts are of no avail.
I asked an old woman in the east about the
    matter
But she wasn't pleased,
And the old fellow in the west
Just frowned and left.
I wrote the problem on a rice cake
And gave it to a puppy
But even it wouldn't bite.
Realizing that such words are bad luck,

I blended life and death into a pill
And gave it to a weather-beaten skull.
The skull suddenly leaped up,
Singing and dancing for me:
A spellbinding ballad that spanned past,
    present, and future,
A marvelous dance that sported through the
    realm of *samsara*.
The skull covered everything most
    thoroughly;
I saw the moon set on Ch'ang-an and heard
    its midnight bells!

Someday I'll be a weather-beaten skull resting
    on a grass pillow,
Serenaded by a stray bird or two.
Kings and commoners end up the same,
No more enduring than last night's dream.

I descended to the valley to gather orchids
But the basin was blanketed with frost and
    dew,
And it took all day to find the flowers.
Suddenly I thought of an old friend
Separated from me by miles of mountains
    and rivers.
Will we ever meet again?
I gaze toward the sky,
Tears streaming down my cheeks.

We meet only to part,
Coming and going like white clouds,
Leaving traces so faint
Hardly a soul notices.

I have an old staff
That has well served many.
Its bark has worn away;
All that remains is the strong core.
I used it to test the waters,
And often it got me out of trouble.
Now, though, it leans against the wall,
Out of service for years.

In a dilapidated three-room hut
I've grown old and tired;
This winter cold is the
Worst I've suffered through.
I sip thin gruel, waiting for the
Freezing night to pass.
Can I last until spring finally arrives?
Unable to beg for rice,
How will I survive the chill?
Even meditation helps no longer;
Nothing left to do but compose poems
In memory of deceased friends.

On the slope of
Kugami,
In the mountain shade,
How many years
Was this hut my home?
Now it is time
To leave it empty—
My memory will fade
Like summer grasses.
Back and forth
I paced around it
And then walked away
Until the hut disappeared
Among the trees.
As I walk, I keep
Looking back after each bend,
Looking back at that place.

I took my staff and slowly made my way
Up to the hut where I spent so many years.
The walls had crumbled and it now sheltered
    foxes and rabbits.
The well by the bamboo grove was dry,
And thick cobwebs covered the window
    where I once read by moonlight.
The steps were overrun with wild weeds,
And a lone cricket sang in the bitter cold.
I walked about fitfully, unable to tear myself
    away
As the sun set sadly.

An Abandoned Hut

Those plum blossoms
We once floated in our wine.
Now the flowers are
Scattered, unnoticed,
All over the ground.

Caged Birds

Time and again
You, too,
Must long for
Your old nest
Deep in the mountains.

Love Poems
between Ryōkan and Teishin

Was it really you
I saw,
Or is this joy
I still feel
Only a dream?

—TEISHIN

In this dream world
We doze
And talk of dreams—
Dream, dream on,
As much as you wish.

—RYŌKAN

Here with you
I could remain
For countless days and years,
Silent as the bright moon
We gazed at together.

—TEISHIN

If your heart
Remains unchanged,
We will be bound as tightly
As an endless vine
For ages and ages.

—RYŌKAN

Have you forgotten me
Or lost the path here?
Now I wait for you

All day, every day.
But you do not appear.

—RYŌKAN

The moon, I'm sure,
Is shining brightly
High above the mountains,
But gloomy clouds
Shroud the peak in darkness.

—TEISHIN

You must rise above
The gloomy clouds
Covering the mountaintop.
Otherwise, how will you
Ever see the brightness?

—RYŌKAN

Chanting old poems,
Making our own verses,
Playing with a cloth ball,
Together in the fields—
Two people, one heart.

The breeze is fresh,
The moon so bright—
Together
Let's dance until dawn
As a farewell to my old age.

Exchange of Poems
on Ryōkan's Deathbed

"When, when?" I sighed.
The one I longed for
Has finally come;
With her now,
I have all that I need.

—RYŌKAN

We monastics are said
To overcome the realm
Of life and death—
Yet I cannot bear the
Sorrow of our parting.

—TEISHIN

Everywhere you look
The crimson leaves
Scatter—
One by one,
Front and back.

        —Ryōkan

My legacy—
What will it be?
Flowers in spring,
The cuckoo in summer,
And the crimson maples
Of autumn . . .

Notes on the Illustrations

THE INK PAINTINGS in the text were created by Koshi no Sengai (Sakuichi Saitō, 1895–1958). Devoting himself to paintings of Ryōkan, the artist passed his days leading a quiet and simple life in the Niigata countryside. Several of the paintings reproduced here include calligraphy of Ryōkan's poems.

p. 9   Gogō-an, Ryōkan's hermitage deep in the woods of Mount Kugami.

p. 139   The nun Teishin. "From heaven/a gift more precious/than jewels or gold:/a visit from you/on the first day of spring!"

SHAMBHALA CENTAUR EDITIONS are named for a classical modern typeface designed by the eminent American typographer Bruce Rogers. Modeled on a fifteenth-century Roman type, Centaur was originally an exclusive titling font for the Metropolitan Museum of Art, New York. The first book in which it appeared was Maurice de Guérin's *The Centaur*, printed in 1915.

Until recently, Centaur type was available only for handset books printed on letterpress. Its elegance and clarity make it the typeface of choice for Shambhala Centaur Editions, which include outstanding classics of the world's literary and spiritual traditions.

ONLY COMPANION
Japanese Poems of Love and Longing
Translated and edited by Sam Hamill

PRAYER OF THE HEART
Writings from the Philokalia
Compiled by St. Nicodemus of the Holy Mountain
and St. Macarios of Corinth
Translated by G. E. H. Palmer, Philip Sherrard, and
Kallistos Ware

THE TALE OF CUPID & PSYCHE
by Lucius Apuleius
Translated by Robert Graves

About the Translator

Zen scholar and Aikido instructor John Stevens has lived in Japan since 1973. He is the author of over a dozen books on Buddhism, Zen, Aikido, and Asian culture, including *The Art of Peace; Three Zen Masters: Ikkyu, Hakuin, and Ryokan; Sacred Calligraphy of the East;* and *Lust for Enlightenment: Buddhism and Sex.*

About the Illustrator

Koshi no Sengai was born in Niigata Prefecture in 1895. Devoting his career to paintings of Ryokan, the artist led a quiet and simple life in the Niigata countryside and died in 1958.